TO BE LANGUAGED THUS

flipped eye publishing
London

To Be Languaged Thus
Barbican Young Poets 2023

First published by flipped eye publishing © 2023
Copyright © 2023, Barbican Centre
Cover Design © 2023, flipped eye publishing
Author Images © 2023, Aiden Harmitt-Williams

All Rights Reserved. The rights of the individual authors to be identified as contributors to this anthology have been asserted in accordance with Section 77 of the Copyright, Designs and Patents Act 1988.

No part of this publication may be reproduced, stored in a retrieval system, or transmitted, in any form or by any means, electronic, mechanical, photocopying, recording, or otherwise, without the written permission of the appropriate individual author, nor may it be otherwise circulated in any form of binding or cover other than that in which it is published and without a similar condition including this condition being imposed on the subsequent purchaser.

This book is typeset in Trajan Pro and Palatino Linotype.

flipped eye publishing
www.flippedeye.net

ISBN-13: 978-1-905233-84-7

To Be Languaged Thus

Barbican Young Poets 2023

barbican

For Gboyega Odubanjo

To Be Languaged Thus
Barbican Young Poets 2023

FOREWORD
Hoor Alnuaimi
   Dollhouse   11
   Self-Portrait as an Everyday Miracle that Refuses to Be Called an
   Everyday Miracle   12
Alex Chand
   Beach   13
   September 12th, 2001   14
Rachel Cleverly
   In Lidl   16
   Project Porcupine   18
Kiara Gilbert
   Love Song from a Black Boy's Bike   19
   My Mother, Beloved as a Ghost Story   20
Marianne Habeshaw
   impulse control   21
   Your neighbour finds breakdown and recovery   22
Charlotte Higgins
   Belfast   25
   Cradle me now in your arms London City   26
   Same boy   27
Rosanna Hildyard
   The pain came and went but here I am invoking it again   28
Oli Isaac
   to whom / it may / concern   30
   you can time-lapse anything to make it seem more significant   32
Asmaa Jama
   ars poetica without resurrection   34
   Ars: Bilaal   36
Tatenda Matsvai
   A (**father**) holds C (**his brother**)   in plastic   40
   The price of milk   42

Sarah McCreadie
   HORROR MOVIE JUMPSCARE — 44
   VHS tape of your third birthday party — 45
Poppy Medenis
   blue — 47
   there is no singing in the dictionary — 48
Francis-Xavier Mukiibi
   On Botany: Things I'd Like to Know — 50
   Ssenga — 51
Robin Park
   bingsu (summer 1999) — 52
   Somehow — 53
Niharika Pore
   | ars diagnosa | — 54
   | bone shlōk | — 56
Riwa Saab
   Homesickness as a cartoon villain — 58
   you are angry at 4AM — 59
Zahrah Sheikh
   Blue — 60
   what every
        body needs — 61
Michael Sookhan
   Moustache Men — 63
   Tender Loving Care — 64
Jinhao Xie
   Am I supposed to be grateful that you donated your seed to Mum? — 65
   Wail — 67
Biographies

FOREWORD

I try to avoid my own clichés and tropes. Nonetheless, the notion of community is one I'll often refer to when speaking about Barbican Young Poets. Each year, while trying (and admittedly sometimes failing) to avoid doling out explicit commandments, I try to cultivate a space in which we can appreciate the benefits of care and attention. Caring for and attending to the work we're here to do, yes. But also caring for the people we share the space with. Those who we work (and play) alongside. How important it is for the individual writer to appreciate their existence in a continuum of others, whether those others be close at hand or separated by distance and time. How we benefit from acknowledging our differences as much as celebrating everything we share. What it means to be an active participant, to give as well as receive. What it means for us to share our successes and losses, however large or small.

One of the programme's key developments in recent years has been a deepening commitment to presentations becoming a core part of the programme's structure. Each presentation provides an insight into themes or elements of craft or practice that members of the cohort are grappling with. Presentations this year ran the gamut from time management, energy management and prioritisation (as offered by Charlotte Higgins) to notes on a pedagogy centred around the value of love in creative practice (as offered by Jinhao Xie). These presentations and others have in various ways fed into the development of much of the work collected within this anthology, as much as any other element of instruction, prompts or feedback.

Sarah McCreadie's HORROR MOVIE JUMPSCARE owes its inception to Oli Isaac and Jess Rahman-Gonzàlez, who together delivered a presentation on interrogating and occupying archetypes and tropes from horror movies. Sarah's poem deftly approaches the horror that can be derived from the distance between present and past selves and the destabilising effect of a perspective shift brought on by time and growing older, with nods to the lore of characters like   Bloody Mary and Candyman. By the end of it all, we're left unsure as to which self is the protagonist, and which is the aggressor. Maeve Slattery, an alumna, returned to deliver a presentation on botany, sparking Francis-Xavier Mukiibi's "On Botany: Things I'd Like to Know", which marries an enquiry into plant life cycles with a vision of urban life characterised by grief, mortality, and darkness. "On Botany..." lands on an unanswered question, highlighting the fact that there are no easy resolutions to the experience Francis-Xavier details. Both of Asmaa Jama's poems owe something to R.A. Villanueva, who as a guest delivered a presentation that concluded with a prompt to draft an ars poetica— to detail the writer's relationship with writing, what the writer values, how the writer falls short, and how the writer sustains their efforts. In Asmaa's's hands, the ars poetica contends with life and afterlife, the necessity and shortcomings of ritual and tradition, the way the voice of the poet is simultaneously personal and peopled. Asmaa does all this through text that inhabits the page with an unassuming dynamism, text that renders the page itself a field of thought.

I'm very aware of how much I lean on and employ the idea of community. What a gift it is to look towards this anthology as a manifestation of that investment. How these poets' active workings have impacted on each other. How members of previous BYP cohorts remain connected as part of the fabric of the larger group that constitutes the community. How that community continues to live and breathe and grow in spite of, and because of, the acts of any individuals.

Jacob Sam-La Rose,
Artistic Director and Lead Facilitator, Barbican Young Poets

Hoor Alnuaimi

Dollhouse
Translated from Arabic, بيت الدُّمى و الدِّماء

There was once a time when it would rain peels.
Garlic, orange, tangerine.

We would gather under her thighs, the tent of the house,
nibbling at skin, looking up at a whole mother
with hands as soft as they were
failing.

And when they would fail,
we would hide away in our doll and blood houses,
eating our little fingers.

Self-Portrait as an Everyday Miracle that Refuses to Be Called an Everyday Miracle

يديها دُعاء، و يد المرأة من عجينٍ و ماءٍ.
A hand is a prayer,
and women's hands are made of dough.
Raising her palms towards her face, she broke
into tears.

The way out is on the left.

She extended her thumb and index finger slowly,
searching for the letter L in her hands, and ever so hesitantly,
followed her body outside the station.

And there she stood,
seven years old and late for school,
wearing her left shoe on her right foot
right shoe on the left,
hands in mouth,
waiting for a miracle.

Alex Chand

Beach

Girl adjusts a double D, too big
for her left tit, fifteen, black straps underneath
a white shirt reading: Lewis and Clark Expedition.

It's not 1865, yet girl rolls her jeans, sprints
to the Pacific, crashing voice in her
stomach. Girl hits her knees to the break

and lifts her eyes. Girl dips her chin below shoreline
practicing a glance her lover has taught after girl
stuffed girlishness into a wire frame.

Detritus. Girl's hair wet like a seagull
gritting El Niño's pulse, tussled
where it meets the shirt; asks how
and if a woman can kiss Sacagawea.

September 12th, 2001

In the morning a severed hand has been
excavated from the rubble, ligaments
twisted and ruptured. There is now a War
on Terror and it does not end here,
outlined in static and pixels inside
the television's frame. Everywhere
satellites broadcast some combination
of these zeros: the ring on the finger,
vessels curled into fists, the ground
collapsing into a hole. Do not enter the portal
to unearth thumbnails of hearts and stock smashed
to oil-covered bits. Once my body
has braced for impact I keep looking
at the wrist dislodged from blood, beat
no longer contained inside
a single body. I worry
about yellow oxygen masks dropping
from the ceiling of a 737
or the sky, where I hope Phillippe Petit
will walk on a wire between two
buildings again without a net, arms out
to steady him as he dances. He sees
two towers and he has to walk, fists
curled around the balancing
pole; hands gripping the length of this wingspan:
a clear morning in Manhattan.
I have run out of images where this
act ends well. The wrist has been severed

and cracked open by a bomb
sailing into the tower on the plane's
underbelly, Terror's Trojan Horse.
The captions on the television take
root under this scene and the smoke; though I
can't yet read the words. My parents flick
off the volume on the 1999
Zenith, fingers pointing at the silence.

Rachel Cleverly

In Lidl

I almost want him
to see me. I am cactus-like
with items, not yet at
the point of rethinking
almost-purchases before putting
almost all of it back. Almost

everyone is in apathetic
disguise. I wasn't thinking
of him when I should or might
have been, given that almost
everyone looked like him.
I had only just thought

I'd seen him in the middle
aisle, which almost
always holds things
I haven't planned for, but
could do with. It hadn't been him,
actually, obviously, but almost.

I do *think* about him
often: e.g. when someone
I'm sleeping with hits me,
or each time I sit on a roof.
My boyfriend has recently
told me I often use e.g.

when I mean i.e. He explained
the distinction, and I'd thought
about him then, too.

When I see him, not almost, but
actually, he is in the queue,
almost at the front,

I am thinking of him and
looking at him, looking like almost
everybody else. I almost want him
to see me, too. He can't: I am too
many people away, holding onto fruit
I am almost ready to put back.

Project Porcupine

The HR Officer has been reporting on herself.

At the end of week one she ranks: productivity (4), satisfaction (4), team relationships (4). She received no handover document, but was advised that keeping things numerical would elicit less pity.

Her predecessor, Project Porcupine's initial creator, had left hurriedly after underperforming in the report. His chart had been consistent (4)s, until he dipped to (3)s, went back up to (5)s. When the company-wide survey was reviewed in the biweekly meeting, the panopticon of data (known internally as 'the breakdown') was displayed on a screen at the back of Room 2. The HR team looked at the dip and felt that organisational nervousness was beginning to take on a fixed design.

Once the predecessor left, the line on the chart looked like an upturned mouth. The graph became a confirmation of good things.

Kiara Gilbert

Love Song from a Black Boy's Bike

        your sister's hands found me, cleaned me
    a lump of tender in the throat   made this rust sparkle
      at the sight of me   you left aching
        only love   to guide these handles
          never lack   us two
      despite so little   will free each other
        whizzing through the streets' soft folds
           the sky a bruising violet
        strangers flinch at   this creaking frame
       your rush of joy   can hold you and more
     exalting any harness   these bolts and brakes all
        keeping you   butterfly pinned
straight-backed instead of   together
swooping forward   marvel at us
wheeled and   flying over the pavement
    wind-rattled   your teeth
your lungs   shiver in the breeze
wheezing   your whoops
    from excitement   generate
   your durag wings behind you   these slabs of concrete
     the stars your beacon to boyhood   your kingdom
      their glimmer can be yours   until streetlights waken
        if you just   from slumber
          take it   don't waste
        this kindness from your sister's palms

My Mother, Beloved as a Ghost Story

piles wooden spoons   in trash cans dreams of
 splinters   growing thorns through tongues
hates knives   once daylight-dreamed a
      demon sliced her fingers
   blood blooming over the countertop

    brushes hands through my closet
          fabric goosebumping her ghost-fingers
tosses my armoire onto a rug   to release
  confetti of comb teeth   and potpourri and starburst
        wrappers stickied with perfume
builds a dollhouse   with vase shards
   she willed   shatter softly on the carpet
        a tender hurricane   she is
my mother –   a story I repeat
         only after dark

Marianne Habeshaw

impulse control

passion is the urge to grope soup cans after the club
in a supermarket. I'm always in a supermarket
more likely a corner shop pacing to find a sweet spot
where my needs get met. whipping tic-tacs in my mouth
pocket-order. on hold again. asking my late adulthood
are there ripe strawberries in my collarbone? does anyone
want to buy my commute's artwork? has anyone here
dried up in a sex room queue? I've done it before
I'll do it again until the clock learns to harmonise
with my dad pulsing in the aisle with the irrigation
equipment I left back at his house my special package
hasn't turned up yet. my collarbone's crop
is both AI and human what's more human
than error? on the second aisle there's sausage-meat
squeezed into sliding fridges waiting for the reduced
section. three soup cans staring at the fallen
indented wanting concrete hard I've done it before
I'll do it again until my toes origami small talk
in record time. all things keeping me alive longer
seem to be unpopular because bureaucracy is right
on this news channel. it's so painfully hard to get
caught up in a new shortage of emails. I need plans
a clean bowling lane to slap guilt down. my inbox
is too full for subtleties. I like how the consistency
of bed sheets is noticed when she stops motherhood
from protesting, and now? I keep a cacti dying
in my bathroom, thorns remain unanswered
my best phobias are more small than they are true
I draft an apology but even artificial palms
can let sunlight wallow in the back street
of a waiting room if they want

Your neighbour finds breakdown and recovery

I

your neighbour crumbles when he's ignored
while the moon capitalises light. he takes pills

for bitterness in a cauliflower fog,
feels high as a migrating bird's beak

but he's done something wrong, to be sized
down with a natural consequence.

warblers fly back into trees. hills shouldered
into rock start haemorrhaging. he wakes

in distant cowpats. as a lump in a truck.
even townspeople have heard of him now

haloed

by shrieks from the puddles of old playgrounds.
he's a suspect for the death of land's edge -

they've already drawn treasure maps
to his breakdown agenda. legend has it

if you stand in the wrong place
you'll lose all your assets.

II

your neighbour is caged in the truck.
his memory won't confess. gloved in glow

he sees a metallic boundary of cars
both relatable and strange. farm animals

scattered like research. all the passengers
are looking at him, repeating an 'h' sound.

do they know he has murdered the horizon?
townspeople say *if you drive past horses*

and don't say 'horse' you're a psychopath
think psychopaths are born that way

but it's often just extreme trauma.
his backdrop changes from moss

to ocean spray at each mouth spasm.
the truck starts again. bumping into

gossipy landmarks, he points at his long face
and sees a horse. calls himself a psychopath.

III

your neighbour is dropped off as a horse
at a city farm. for work in a stable. innards

like stone sucked in. he chews back hay
and arguments on whether north

is still where it was. he might escape
with tagged sheep between his thighs, but doesn't

keep any of his brain's sentiments. there's a gap
in the stable, he's out in the lake. his tail

finds kindness like a pinpoint. for the first
time in months, he's free from onlookers,

seasoned by rain, loving hypothermia
like a crab overturned in excited tragedy.

sees a week inside of him, or a year
but time out of order and expiry stickers

mixed up on a pile of pebbles. he curves
to sort them with the inner moss of his hooves.

out drip the days. a stream of time in order.

The italicised text is drawn from Maggie Smith's "Poem Beginning With A Retweet" and "Even-Keeled and At-Eased" by Alberto Ríos respectively.

Charlotte Higgins

Belfast

was Diet Coke cans and 20p paper bags of sweets
twisted from the old shop on the corner
we would eat them with cold hands by City Hall
too young yet to have anywhere to go

as the sun set
the last leaves whispering to the ground
I thought *even they fall slow*

Belfast was dark winter nights and the pubs' soft glow
we'd watch as crystal women and basalt men
bustled in the open doors and out again
doorways lined up like headstones in a row

we'd walk home late beside the Lagan's absolute dark
the Christmas-time lights flickering like snow

Cradle me now in your arms London City

i
we walk silent over the Thames and back
miles above the water
flowing like the ghosts in that old Eliot poem

it is a little after sunset
and the city air bites iron-cold
I hear that song my Nana loved – *show me the way to go home*

ii
the lights are off in the corner store
the one with the one pound five pence Diet Cokes
a sign in the window says *we will be back next week, but for now we are closed*

the dictionary definition of falling
is to move from a higher to a lower level
often rapidly and often without control

iii
every morning for months I've walked to work through the cemetery
autumn leaves like offerings at the foot of each headstone
and I think *darling, let's fall a little slower*

the Christmas lights are flickering like candles in the dark
like a whisper that the year is almost over

Same boy

I talk about you to a friend
one I haven't seen in years

same boy? he asks –
and you are
even now we are married and thirty

and ten years away from those nights in the theatre bar
when I would host and you would take the tickets on the door
and walk me home along the river
until it looked like it was filled with stars

the same boy
I'm glad you are

Rosanna Hildyard

The pain came and went but here I am invoking it again

Pale green corridors unribboning in front of you
You have passed Go *Collect*
two hundred pounds Turn left for endocrinology
right for radiology A trio of ghostly nurses

springs out of the dead end Pain
in the ditch of your elbow snatches your attention
Hide in the lift while the nurses pass
They want you hungry your blood sugar-free

but you're sure you saw a Pret a Manger somewhere in here
Leapfrog a floor duck under a gurney
Weave past the other endings in other rooms
The nurses want you in bed tested

but they are rude about your veins and you would miss your turn
At last you are at Pret You have reached safety
It is normal and maroon
Choose a chicken and avocado sandwich

Keep not-looking at your spongy arm
But when you take the sandwich

  nothing
No portal no disappear

You are alone green floors bustling
The game is not over you are still here.
Like, whose fault is this? God?
Genes? Ancestry? It doesn't

matter   Keep playing
stay close to winning   close but not knowing
the mystery of   your own secrets
the results   the nurses' news

Oli Isaac

to whom / it may / concern

apologies for my belated response, but i hope this finds you
the templates i use in emails are spilling into real-life conversations
it's easier sometimes than stumbling over words

please confirm or respond or let me know
my google calendar informs me that tomorrow is the first time you will have
    doubts
do i RSVP or... ?

just a friendly reminder
that the heart on average weighs 300 grams
that coffee can supplement a sense of purpose
that charon's obol is perched on the ledge of my throat

i'm worried i'm coming across too formal
i mean — i look forward to and appreciate this opportunity

don't hesitate if
        the telephone wires tangled between us stretch and fray and lose
            their definition
                unspoken words preserved next to sidewalk gum

to be honest or to be fair or to be
looking for a night that ends with a promise
that things will start again on the first bus home

i look at you and
please come before the offer runs out
brands are always first to wish me a happy birthday

i regret to inform you that your
soft eyes drag me away from knowing
that the blood sloshing around inside me
is only held in by clenched lips and closed fists

i would like to wake up next to you
but no worries if not

i mean — i would love to see spring with you
i mean — i would love to hear back

i have a recycling bin that i keep trying to empty
but it always tells me everything is in use
that everything is always in use

you can time-lapse anything to make it seem more significant

we met at the surprise birthday party for the friend we didn't know
at the house we had to ask strangers to find
two blocks down   you won't miss it

we hid with everyone else   half-drunk drinks forming bruises on tabletops
arms in view from the side of the curtain   legs hanging out from under the bed

we didn't know who to wish happy birthday to
so we stayed behind when everyone else jumped out   when the party ended
when the friend moved

we lingered listening   to new housewarmings and answer phone messages
to debates on whether to tip the driver
to people building homes out of the wrong parts of each other

you said   my lips look bruised

    i said   *it was the wine*

you said   you were a fan of chasing tides   of wading-but-then-running in waist-deep water that
it reminded yourself of your body   until your legs got used to the extra weight

    i said   *it was the wine*

we eventually came out from behind the curtains   wished the wrong person happy birthday   raided the medicine cabinet   camped out in the hallway with backs against radiators like we lived in a nineties american sitcom where our problems had ad-breaks and you couldn't skip forward

we rested on pillows formed out of our hands   i knew then your insides were made of marshmallows and sun-soaked sand   you said in a way that didn't move your mouth *i lied, you know, i'm not a pisces*   i nodded   buried my secrets in your teeth   i swear i marked each one with an x

Asmaa Jama

ars poetica without resurrection

the poem is the liquid cemetery   i dive in, searching mouth
holding the english words   for loss, lost.

if the language has also atrophied, if the child began writing in
ink to reach them, who is to tell them, swapping the vials of the
embalming fluid with ink, it will not revive them.

let it be the mosque – man at the centre of it, white cap on his
head, crochet facing mecca, let it be the mosque

saying   *prophet move*
         angel yell
                : *read,*
and so we did, do, have always done.

after they crossed the liquid strait, they cut off the ghost flesh –
your parents – cut their losses, their old language sank

decomposed, what you are able to resuscitate will not outlive
you, will not outlast your home – your own brother misses
most of the syllables.

you can make only ten perfect sounds. the old poets whittle
astral images in a hundred.

are they speaking in whistles? asks your great-uncle-now-also-
dead. the language of birds —
english so hollow it is the language of birds,

i want to bury the feathers and the evidence of them, what my
tongue knows: how to commit a massacre, how to build a burial
pit, how to burn the record after, build a monument

      after

they had to move, taking   not stone, but tongue,
      figurative and wet,
               a wetter world

my people descend into and i go looking for them

      — what is a gil-less fish?
         '   — guileless.

what if   i can't swim ?   speak ?   sing?

      no longer remember?

the child writes reams around the cadavers and calls it a prayer,
forgets it, mosque, the twelve hours every weekend, how the
sun grew weak, what we were busy with,

prayer-soaked and still too illiterate —

they said the book will empty itself one day,
remember it all, any way you can—

burnt archive, barely contained, battered body, my father had a
crop full of hair once and pushed us on a swing, my
grandmother owned a shop that took two buses to get to.

what is the writing then ?
               my weakness, my crib sheet, my
memory stain, blacked palm, evidence i can't hold it in,
        it
spills,
my hands wet with the words, i try

to transcribe for each of my dead. i know they won't yield to any.

Ars: Bilaal

Bilaal: First utterance

Maybe you exist in the hushed bathwater in the kingdom of domesticity.

We are all paupers and kings - waiting for a prophecy to shake us. God says unbury the girls and you are forced to pull sod from behind their teeth - they spit mineral and sing, each body a minaret - a vast vast chasm, sound spinning upwards.

God says unbury the widows and you do - the old women loose themselves of their wombs and slip back their skin.

Women will have inheritances. God booms and you obey. You can drink your liquor and you obey. Desperate and drunk your tongue slips Al lat, you crash into the carpet.

You can no longer drink. God decrees and you relent. Blood earnestly wanting its siren song. You stand emptied in prayer.

You will not all make it through, God whispers. And you relent - staying up at night watching women split watermelons before the sun rises. So what if you burn, you can't all be beloved. You let the wine rot you.

You watch the sahaba free another slave. This time pulling a stone off a man's chest. You can hear the air re-   entering his lungs. The lungs of a diver - his name is Bilaal.

Bilaal : Second utterance

I am black in a place where black means gone. Disappeared ink.

They have a need for a call. I have tried my tongue at their
marks - fitting it to the grooves of the letters - ink tracing ink.
I swallowed most of them.

الله

was simplest so full, so saviour-   like

شوف   اسمعني

these marks were the same ش س
one flecked, the other empty, but my tongue wouldn't fold- I
pronounced them both *seen* because I wanted to be sighted.
Witnessed, understood. I wanted past tense / a history where it
happened + happens. I am personned and commonplace.

Some of them wanted me gone or to give up the ghost.

Or to return to the shadows

But the prophet said my seen would lead everyone into the sight of God —

Bilaal: third utterance

Tatenda Matsvai

A (*father*) holds C (*his brother*) in plastic

as lightly as a bible
raised to perspex partition

A (*father*)
   names the swollen jaws
   names the bloodied bodies
   names the hospital gowned men   (*his brother*)
by land
by god

A (*father*)
must make an exhibit
for B (*child*) to stay B (*child*)

B must
unsee
   crushed metal
   scorched red brick
   spider smoke licked
   arms braided into wave
    into knot
    into ___

to remain   B (*child*)
must ___

A (*father*) and D (*whose job it is
to grant or deny right to remain*),
do not blink

As A (*father*) slides C (*his brother*)
through a letter box
for evidence

D carries C
  the weight of bodies
  paper thin
to be copied

As if bodies contorted in this way

The price of milk

you haul leather around flank for market
don heel instead of cloven hoof
tits tolling down cement stairs
bare tempting with bare flesh
                 fall

a broken commandment
on your knees   you know
only blood can save you

tell your mother
you were praying

tits couldn't save you
the blood's already spoiled   turned black grey
                 swell

dance finger across stitches prayerfully
spit salvation
sleep
starve desire
let it graze when the house is empty
fingers circling

next week [a girl] names your ear
a house of worship

[she] kisses hard temples under your shirt
tongue searching for [   ]
   [   ] wasn't home

only hands
only tongue

Sunday
you picture [church pianist] playing your back
[He] has perfect pitch
imagine
the hymns [he'd] make of your orgasms

Oh God, Oh God
Oh God, Oh God, he plays

you search [his] notes/[her] legs/ yourself
for [God]
while pastor preaches
wishing you were [God]
instead of the [cow] your father warned you about

make your desires a whisper
between amens like a good
                    girl

Sarah McCreadie

HORROR MOVIE JUMPSCARE

My fifteen year old self appears behind me in the mirror
Did I say *Clearasil* three times to conjure her?
I know those sad eyes and bad glasses
Loose clothes and closet key in pocket
The one who still walks into the room before me
A grin at my life now
The way I say my name
My happiness
I take a step towards me
Snare pole in hand

VHS tape of your third birthday party

in which your grandfather arrives
a third of the way through

the last piece of evidence
that you loved him like that

squint at the static threads for
the smell of his shed or the bend in his back

or how he wore his cap or the look on the face
of the child that is you, running towards him

known through a camcorder
at grown-up height

summer dress
and when was the last time you wore a dress?

e.t. doll hanging in small hands
brushing petticoat-sock ankles

standing next to a yellow slide
and tantrum cousin nobody speaks to anymore

you won't press play
because it might be the last time

and it reminds you
that everything must have a last time

night terrors of tape guts
machine death

lump in the throat at all this
being swallowed

a tape or the black spot
when you close your eyes

was your grandfather late
at the railway club with the other old men

when you saw him last
you were the only one in the room

breathing

Poppy Medenis

blue

the first time
nanny reyner flew
she was 75
into the blue
so disappointed
as she saw
above the clouds
there was no heaven
up there
just water
there's so much
more joy
in faith
i look up
to the blue
and wonder
where she is now
imagining
that heaven
is right here
this sky
this sun
singing
to my skin

there is no singing in the dictionary

not even in hope:

a feeling of expectation and desire
for a particular thing to happen.

i hear october leaves
praying for their lives
lukewarm bath water
shared between the 4 of us

the taste
of chasing arrival.

what if
i am the bruised 89p mango
in corner shop basket
and hope is being cradled by your hands

there is no space for scatting,
there is no song in expectation's edges

hope is in the knowing

humming
at last my love has come along
as you wash round taps
and clean shit off shoe

the pressure of your thumb
between spine and shoulder blade

hope in the running of the bath water that will wash us all
the mango that will be cut into segments
enough to feed 500

no   hope is not
in the purple of desire
it lives in the bruise

Francis-Xavier Mukiibi

On Botany: Things I'd Like to Know

How much germinates in one space? Do you, like us, feel intrusion?

> We plant hairdressers: Mirror light paths.
> Clipper chord grips. Olive seeds. Hands
> sprout plastic tips. Our lips–moths mixing
> tongues, crossbreeding generations.

The sun doesn't stay out. How much do your bodies cope at night?

> Red light to spotlight. Oil to rum spilt. Siren to
> fandom. Our silhouettes fight horrors. Day is
> a stagnant lens–in dark, we lose inhibition.

How much longer would your juveniles live if left by powers that be?

> Drop boydem's cloak, reveal him
> washing-line-thin. We vessels hold cloud
> when tranquil, smoke when tried. Boydem's
> baton is porcelain-turned-wheat upon strike.

How much are you accustomed to being fed bodies of your dying?

> Through leather palms: Pluck screams of
> grieving fathers. Grip them. The layers split.
> Our dying aren't war. They're warning.

Your language to us: a perennial silence. How much has this cost?

Ssenga

Ssenga holds silence
in the corners where tears once were. To forget
is to remove herself from that which
roots her. How damaging
                              to shift, detach
                      from the spines holding her
to the worms out back in the compound; her father's
                          fathers long since devoured.
His name is
mentioned without cracks,
the tombstone of her uvula already shifted,
    its surrounding earth falling,
                        feeding sweet banana stem,
                                matooke peelings
                        where she sits, browning
            on the concrete. Does she see herself
in the ailing fruit wrapped under leaves,
steaming, mouldered soft? The spines
do not allow her to break
yet; this body
too whole
to crumple.   In the compound,
                    taatas sit on mukeekas–
        flaking at the wailing threads. Ssenga holds
            plates of matooke; the weight of bone
                china pulses at her fingertips.

Robin Park

bingsu (summer 1999)

the only reason to stand
    this city-heat is to stir-boil

        the red beans: bubbling
            starch-sweet & mountainous

    mother takes a basin
        full of ice & churns out

layered flakes
    arms slick with humidity

        the two of us condensing
            into monsoon-thick air

            I open the canned milk
        & dribble it down the hill of ice

        watch it gather
        at the bottom of the glass

    I pool at the base of myself
into a girl-shaped vessel

        mother heaps a ladleful
    of red bean & gently tops

        the sugar snow: I take two
    spoons & fold it all together

Somehow

The islands are disappearing. Just like eggs from grocery shelves & gas pipes as they burst beneath the sea. How can I drive along another coastline & not imagine my car slipping under – swallowed by an expanding Earth-mouth? The light blushes pink in the crevices of Laurel Canyon, oblivious of satellite debris above & a missile strike across the Pacific, loud enough to drown out the cry of another mother. There is so much splintering – beneath our feet, in our lungs, through the ice sheets, in the body of fish. I scroll through my feed & click on an ad for another floral maxi dress I will not wear. I buy that $9 smoothie in Melrose & try to eclipse the image of drought-singed bushes by the freeway exit ramp. Drink orange wine & holiday in Mallorca in the era of war-plague alliance. Everyday, I anticipate a final curtain & it does not fall.

Niharika Pore

| ars diagnosa |

                      i hatched from the bump in her sternum.
      having resided   unspoken, in   convulsive
sputterances   — blue-tongued as i am   i seeped
     slowly through bonecracks leaving   eggshell trails
        until   .

                now,

          she picks at the calcified   remains
of me,   shuddering in ecstasy   and swabs at the cavity.

          sequence me!   i cry, and wait to be
                found,

          a flash   — luminosity itself,
    we gaze through x-ray windows   glimpsing the
spaces   i left behind.   she's forgotten my name, again.
     but   she wonders sometimes if the wine-sick bruises
          in the pits of her wrists that   flare
              enraged,

        at merementions of another   needle
or heatwave,   might be remnants of a lost friend.

             after all,

                 i've portraited myself after her long-dead
        sister, sitting   intercostal for an age.   lacrimal,
we might have flowed out together   but she
         had to leave and i   left to cocoon, an infesting of
                rust-crumbled leather,   what might have been

                                and

                           i know i can be painful.
                                 her fingers

                                   twist,

                     away   from me
              dustings of disused nutmeg grey her musculature,
        ashen   on her bed of nails, maltbrown   soaking deep
                into   the floorboards under her fat —
                      oh,   how i'd love to atrophy me.

                to be languaged thus   — languidly, i
        lick the inside of her cheek to find   the chewed-up bridge
                    waiting   to be spat.

                                  dosed,

                    i feel nauseatingly prescribed,
             i'll sleep at the base of her skull, one more time
         just once   before i'm found/   ripped/   studied/
                      removed from her,   diagnosed.
                                i'll shriek —

| **bone shlōk** |

      an epidermis so
full of creatures that one might mistake
   you for a rotten log
       he laughs and demands you find comfort in
cosmos or haldi   you're suspended
anyways   swimsuit on to shield
    from his spitty fallacies of
medical excellence   or free coffee.

with salt between your eyes   blink
    lest rākshas be
summoned. after all
   you have to trust the gods! trust
     their plans for your pain.
they'll declare you a lost
      cause without a future or ribcage
decrying you   sick
     your horrid muscles to fill with
   wasps   *infestation that you are.*

    and without a thought you
end up going home in
   the back of his
  vauxhall corsa on the way home
pissing outside
      vauxhall station   leaving your body
stationed   knowing you've never
   had a real body anyway.

he'll save you
    a seat at the
surgical table
      your reflection striping his
          paan-red smile
eight-pronged fork in your throat   dripping
  tar on tongues   folded
      a new cup for him to sip from.
he'll feast
      gleaming with ferrous intent
  the way he always was.

Riwa Saab

Homesickness as a cartoon villain

The hyena at Green Park laughs at your picnic meal deal choices, imitates your mother tongue, asks why you betrayed it when you quit being nocturnal.   *Will we ever meet again?*

It doesn't have eyebrows to raise to tell you 'no.' It laughs, says there's no bus from here that takes you home, only to the pharmacy or the pub, and you're neither sick nor sober.

How many features can I hide before the camera tries to hold me captive? My love, I was never here to begin with, only passing.

you are angry at 4AM

in the night, behind the thin wall we keep between us,
i hear a thump and a squawk, and i think, how painful
it must be to turn into a bird in the middle of this heated
summer evening, to grow quills and plumes out of your
follicles and tuck yourself back into bed, as if nothing ever
happened, or as if you were meant for anything other than
flight.

Zahrah Sheikh

Blue

The chemist Heinz Berke notes humans "had no access to blue because blue is not what you call an earth colour, you don't find it in soil"
— True blue: a brief history of the color blue in art, Carol Burns

A colour that exists forever or what forever looks at
    or towards from this shoreline.
It rolls as a marble believes it can spin away grief
Pigment clings to the brush, doesn't want to be an imitation of rain.
It is my ceiling, the ground I skim my feet on, the breath of lapis lazuli
    knocking at my toe

lapis meaning stone   *lazuli* blue

In the blue that holds you   I will swim through stone to reach you

what every body needs

understanding is love's other name
  - Thich Nhat Hanh

"I don't know love's first
name but I know its second

& maybe
that's all I need."

The ant survives the wave,
    buries the earthquake

        with its leg.

Lists all the sweaters it wants
to wear, the different types
of warmth
to feel.

It boils light,

    presses a wing to its back.

        Devours the skin

off Icarus's back.

It touches the sky like a promise

& whispers
> *let me know you*

Michael Sookhan

Moustache Men

We didn't talk much.

Bonded more over murder,
smashing controllers
at the back of the net.

Now you're a father.

And the lost brother in the supermarket has a beard like a wisdom tooth.

Tender Loving Care

You're useless
Where did you put it boy?
Answer me
Stupid boy
Listen
If you hit someone, it's self defence
Boy

> Do you need a hand?
> Cup of tea?
> Newspaper?
> This is how you send a text
> Good to see you too, Dad

Jinhao Xie

Am I supposed to be grateful that you donated your seed to Mum?

After "I Go Back to May 1937"- Sharon Olds

I go back to the heat of Kai Ping in 1983. New Year's Eve simmers.
A distant cousin ran home barefoot, firecrackers whipped
the side of your foot.

you were supposed to be boybrave,
a fist-thumping-on-your-chest kind of innocence
while other boys chanced their lives with the Pearl River –

January, merciless, moon,
the neon-lit harbour breaming with temptations,
                harvesting young promises & labourers –

1983 – an improbable year for us to meet. But I see you
squatting on a three-legged stool,
Lucky Strike embering between your index & thumb,
your starved jaws & smoking –

you were supposed to be a good swimmer –
you were supposed to be in Hong Kong, lying
on the beach; swollen &
pale like a beached sperm whale –

supposed to be the end of a family line –
instead, with all this poetry, here
I am – fucking
boys & fucking
girls & this fucking
alive & –

Love?

Am I supposed to be grateful?

Wail

Now, they want us to speak. Ears gaze into this abyss of us. Crosshoders, pearlclutchers and belief divers. So deep we are. This linguistics. Sea. Listen. After we saved their (female) sailors, their children, and their men, after they burnt us for holiness and happiness and hope. Candles aren't innocent. Now, they've invented this device to hear us. The unreachable frequencies. They singsong, *we can hear you*. In their own words, they want to know our thoughts, our desires. After blooding our kins. *How did you wail for your mothers?* Mother saw this coming – oracles etched in our fins – that there would be a day, they would come for us: wonder how on this earth we lived for this long, sing our songs and ask why our tears filled this whole ocean. *Where did you begin?* We sing nothing. We stare back at them with the same-shaped eyes as theirs. Oculi Hominis. Horror flashes on their faces, white bubbles, choking. We wail with such glee, *let's bathe amongst those white-washed faces.*

so bright! so damn bright!

Biographies

Hoor Alnuaimi [9]
Hoor is a graduate student at the University of Oxford and an emerging writer and translator, currently working on completing a bilingual novella in Arabic and English that explores the different objects in Emirati women's quotidian lives. She is interested in the relationship between language, violence, and womanhood, and hopes to continue navigating these themes in her work at the Barbican. Hoor is based in Abu Dhabi, U.A.E.

Alex Chand [4]
From California, Kentucky, and Texas, Alex Chand is currently studying English Literature at the University of Leeds on a Fulbright. Most recently Alex competed at UniSlam on the University of Leeds team in 2023, finishing second, and was named a finalist for the William S. Robe Playwriting Residency. In 2022, Chand graduated with a BA from Lawrence University in physics and English, where she was awarded the Didderich Prize in Creative Writing and earned summa cum laude honours for her thesis, Charting Autistic Voices. You can find Alex on the web at https://alexchand.com.

Rachel Cleverly [1]
Rachel Cleverly is a poet and producer. She is an Old Vic Theatre Maker and an alumnus of Apples and Snake's 'The Writing Room' and BBC Words First. She has an MA in Creative Writing Poetry from the University of East Anglia, and has been shortlisted for the UEA New Forms Award, commended in the Winchester Poetry Prize, and published by flipped eye publishing, The North, SPAM, ACHE Magazine and The Feminist Library among others. Rachel works as an Education Officer at The Poetry Society, where she manages the Foyle Young Poets of the Year Award. You can find out more about Rachel on her website www.rachelcleverly.com and on Twitter & Instagram @rachel_cleverly

Kiara Gilbert [5]

Kiara Gilbert is a graduate student at the intersection of ethics, political theory, and African American Studies. Her research is rooted in the lived experiences and philosophies of Black American communities. She graduated with a BA in African American Studies from Princeton University and an MPhil in Criticism and Culture from the University of Cambridge. She recently co-published a chapter on Black revolutionary Frederick Douglass in Rethinking Political Theory, published by Oxford University Press.

Marianne Habeshaw [10]

Marianne Habeshaw is a queer, East London-based poet from Peterborough and an artist in residence at St. Margaret's House. She is a teaching assistant and also curates, produces and performs at an annual collaborative poetry event at St. Margaret's house. Her goal is to provide other emerging artists with a platform to workshop and experiment with new work while building community. She loves poems that locate her emotionally, especially when she doesn't know what's going on. Marrianne's had two poems 'The Theories of Porky Pig' and 'Your neighbour finds breakdown and recovery' longlisted for the Outspoken Prize for page poetry in 2023. Her poem 'An Imperfect Love Story' was longlisted for the Outspoken Prize for page poetry in 2022. She was awarded a Free Reads Scheme in 2021 for her collection 'Blather Gaps.' Between 2019 to 2021, published by the LADA website, Unseen Words and Visuals and Enthusiastic Press. She wrote a play with Eastern Angles in 2019 called 'Snowflakes in the Slow cooker' (about culture wars and political opposition in Britain) and was commissioned by Paines Plough in 2020.

Charlotte Higgins [3]

Charlotte Higgins is a poet from Belfast, now based in London. She has been writing and performing for over 10 years - and has performed poetry at Glastonbury, Latitude, the Proms, Ledbury Poetry Festival, the Nuyorican Poetry Café, and on Radio 3. She is a previous winner of SLAMbassadors and the Foyle Young Poets of the Year award.

Rosanna Hildyard [2]
Rosanna Hildyard is an editor and writer from North Yorkshire. She is an alumnus of the Roundhouse Poetry Collective. Her poetry and fiction has recently been published in Salt's Best British Short Stories, Vittles, PERVERSE, Banshee and Modern Poetry in Translation, been shortlisted for the Benedict Kiely Award and come second in the Brick Lane Short Story Prize. Her short story pamphlet, Slaughter, was longlisted for the Edge Hill Prize in 2021 and is available from Broken Sleep Books.

Oli Isaac [6]
Oli Isaac is a London-based playwright and poet, who likes to write tender poems about their tender thoughts. Having grown up with a stutter, they are interested in how language can fail us + how experiments in poetry and multimedia can attempt to cross that gap. Oli is a recipient of Audible Theatre's Emerging Playwrights Fund and has previously been selected as a lead artist for the Barbican x CRIPtic showcase and the BBC's Word's First festival. They are an alumni of Soho Theatre Writers' Lab, Roundhouse Poetry Collective and the Apples & Snakes' Writing Room.

Asmaa Jama [13]
Asmaa Jama is a Somali interdisciplinary artist and writer based in Bristol. Jama has been commended by the Brunel African Poetry Prize and shortlisted for the Wasafiri Writing Prize, James Berry Prize, New Poets Prize and Outspoken Page Poetry Prize and longlisted in the National Poetry Competition. Jama is a Cave Canem Fellow. Asmaa has been published in anthologies and in print, and has been translated into Somali, Swahili, French, German and Portuguese. As a film director, Asmaa was commissioned by BBC Arts to make the interactive film Before We Disappear (2021), and by Bristol Old Vic to make The Season of Burning Things (2021), which was screened at the 17th Venice Biennale of Architecture (2021), as part of 100 Ways to say We and at Art Basel, Hong Kong. Asmaa's upcoming solo exhibition, with collaborator Gouled Ahmed, for a new moving image work, Except this time nothing comes back from the ashes will open at Spike Island, Bristol in June. In theatre, Asmaa has collaborated with choreographers Radouan Mrziga (Akal) and Dorothee Munyaneza

(Mailles). And has performed and toured in Mailles, over the past two years, in venues such as the Pompidou Centre, Paris. Asmaa has held residencies at Callie's, Berlin and with Onassis Stegi, (Alexandria, Marseille and Athens). And is a fellow with Film London, and a current resident artist at Somerset House Studios.

Tatenda Matsvai [7]

Tatenda Naomi Matsvai (aka 2tender) is a facilitator and devised performance maker, working with spoken word poetry in theatrical and non-theatrical performance contexts. Tatenda's work is mainly bio-mythical, infusing their lived experience with myth, to challenge colonial cosmologies. Their performances are joyful, participatory, and multidimensional. They are currently developing their co-written show Hot Orange with Halfmoon Theatre. Tatenda's work has won the Vault Origins award, been Offie nominated, and performed as part of Theatre Peckham, The Roundhouse Camden, The Cockpit for Voila Europe! festival and Between. Pomiędzy Festival (Poland).

Sarah McCreadie [18]

Sarah McCreadie is a poet, performer and lesbian heart-throb from Cardiff and has performed her poetry from Newport to New York. Her poetry was published in 2022 by flipped eye publishing in the anthology Articulations for Keeping the Light In and by Y Lolfa in Wal Goch - Ar Ben y Byd. She was named as one of Craig Charles' Poets of 2022'. Sarah is a BBC 1Xtra 'Words First' poet and former resident artist at the Roundhouse theatre. Her collaborations range from Vanity Fair to Match of the Day. You can find Sarah online on Twitter at @Girl_Like_Sarah, hear her poems on Youtube or come watch her at a show!

Poppy Medenis [8]

Poppy Medenis is a London-based designer who engages with the question of what a poem can be considered as: conversation, song, textiles or the act of making itself. She explores themes of faith, hope and everyday beauty through song, poetry, printmaking and photography. She is most inspired by the poets that haven't been named as so, and believes there is a book in every person. Through running creative workshops in hospitals, community centres and schools she encourages people to celebrate their unique voices.

Francis-Xavier Mukiibi [19]
Francis-Xavier Mukiibi (@fxmpoetry) is a poet and spoken word performer of Ugandan heritage from North London. He is an alumnus of the Roundhouse Poetry Collective and the Obsidian Foundation retreat. He has performed his poetry on BBC Radio and iPlayer and has also featured in various creative arts festivals throughout London and the Midlands, including Festival2Funky in Leicester, the Camden Inspire Festival, and the Roundhouse Last Word Festival. His poetry appears in Ink Sweat & Tears, Zindabad Zine and Under the Radar by Nine Arches Press.

Robin Park [11]
Robin Park is a Korean-American poet based in the UK. Her poems often contain glimpses of her family and attempts to make sense of her own nomadic identity. She is currently exploring the concept of randomness, both in her creative process and in her poems. She was an inaugural member of the Southbank Centre's New Poets Collective.

Niharika Pore [15]
Niharika Poré is a multidisciplinary writer, artist, and curator working across several cultural institutions and community groups through London. They build sensory moments for the reader, reflecting on personal experiences of disability, diaspora, and queerness. Working with metaphors of ecology and speculative fiction, they worldbuild to capture dissociated memories through distanced perspectives. They also explore installation and sculptural form with printed text, making reading spaces within which to become lost.

Riwa Saab [16]
Riwa Saab is a London-based artist who works with space, sound, and words. By braiding together the crafts of poetry, theatre, and music, she interrogates how art puts people and our relationships at the centre of the political narratives we inhabit, while particularly exploring the diasporic

experience of building cultural bridges, unpacking generational and familial baggage, and creating space for pockets of joy.

Zahrah Sheikh [17]

Zahrah Sheikh, a British Pakistani poet from Ilford. Her writing mainly explores prayer, the self, the weight of an action and silence.

Michael Sookhan [12]

Michael is a Barbican Young Poet and theatre maker.

Jinhao Xie [14]

Jinhao Xie is a member of Southbank Centre New Poets Collective. Their work is in POETRY, Poetry Review, Harana, Bath Magg, Gutter Magazine and and anthologies, including Articulations for Keeping the Light In, Slam! You're Gonna Wanna Hear This edited by Nikita Gill, Instagram Poems for Every Day by National Poetry Library, Fourteen Poems and Re.Creation. They are the inaugural champion of Asia House Poetry slam 2018. They are interested in nature, the mundane, the interpersonal and selfhood.